My Tao Te Ching: A Fools Guide to Effing the Ineffable

Francis Briers

"Francis Briers has done a brilliant job of casting the Tao Te Ching into a modern and popular form. His rendition flows with a humour and innocence that truly reflect the essence of the Taoist tradition. Whether you are approaching philosophy and personal development for the first time, or are an experienced explorer, My Tao Te Ching will make you smile with its wry insights and encourage you to be at ease with the wondrous miracle and paradox of your life."

- William Bloom, PhD, and author 'The Power of Modern Spirituality: How to Live a Life of Compassion and Personal Fulfilment'

"I'm happy to have introduced Francis to the 'Tao Te Ching' as his Kung Fu Instructor many years ago and watched his progress over the years. To take on this 'bible' of Taoism could be an onerous task but Francis has the insight, wisdom and humour to make it work. It's an excellent and accurate translation with the wit and humour to keep any normal person engaged and able to understand the original meaning of the text with those deep 'glimpses' that can only come from true understanding."

- Steve Rowe, 8th Dan Karate, International Tai Chi Teacher, Chairman of the Martial Arts Standards Agency and Shi Kon Martial Arts International

"A beautiful book which touches on the wonderful, mysterious and sometimes ridiculous nature of life, the universe, and everything. Wonderful, creative and enjoyable!"

- Sue Cheshire, CEO and Founder, Global Leaders Academy

"...the belly laughs start and they come in waves throughout the book, sometimes full blown waves of laughter as I recognise in myself the wanting to take myself and life too seriously, and sometimes the laughter is more subdued as I own the parts of me that do not want to let go ... Each chapter is a meditation helping us not to be so grasping, to empty ourselves so that love and compassion can flow through us, without interference. The style of writing is like love poetry and reminds me of the poetry of the many mystical traditions - Such a gift. "

- Dr. Josie Gregory, PhD, and Director of The Centre for Spiritual Development and Facilitation

"In this version of the Tao Te Ching, Francis Briers has brought to us a unique, playful, humorous, contemporary, and relevant edition of this well of delights. I find it a helpful, practical, and, at points, very funny read. Making a traditional text live in the modern world like this provides a valuable resource to us busy bees."

- Luke Concannon, No.1 hit musician and activist

Also by Francis Briers:

A Little Book on Finding your Way –
Zen and the Art of Doing Stuff

Warrior Philosophy in Game of Thrones

The Little Book of Appreciation

And coming soon...

Radical Embrace: Integrating
Leadership, Embodiment, Compassion &
Sustainability

Compassion For The Earth –
Sustainability as an act of loving
kindness

The Wisdom Economy

My Tao Te Ching:

A Fools Guide to Effing the Ineffable

Please note that the author accepts no liability for any effing done on the part of the reader. Whether this book has inspired it or not, your effing is entirely your responsibility.

Warriors of Love Publishing

ISBN: 978-0-9567799-3-9

A copy of this book has been deposited with the British Library.

Published by Warriors of Love (WOL) Publishing

CONTENTS

A Fool's Guide to Effing the Ineffable

Introduction: Why re-write a classic of Chinese philosophy?

Flavour. That's the short answer. I'm not an academic who can bring a striking new perspective to the translation of the ancient Chinese language, I'm a practitioner. Having lived, loved and practiced various Taoist arts over the last 15 years or so, and having done my best to absorb and express the teaching of the Tao Te Ching I've come to love what this text has to offer. Through its poetry, I feel I have been given a glimpse of the underlying patterns of the world I live in, a hint at what the infinite and divine feel like. I want to share that glimpse as best as I can to as many people as want to hear, see, feel, or live it.

I've read more than a dozen different translations of the Tao Te Ching over the years and regularly refer to 4 versions. But even in the versions I like best and which have so wonderfully captured the poetry and mystery which I'm sure inhabit the original text, I feel something is missing. In many of the stories of Taoist teachers, their students, and even their Gods, there is a sense of humour. There is an acknowledgement of the ultimate foolishness in all human endeavours, the wondrous insignificance of mankind, and the peace and wisdom to be gained from laughing at all the paradoxical experiences that life throws at us.

"Life doesn't make sense again, how hilarious!"

It is not a cynical rejection of the world, standing at a distance within myself laughing at the world 'out there'; it is a total commitment to being entirely immersed in the world, human nature, and all its attendant pains and difficulty, while maintaining the capacity to find joy in witnessing my own foolishness and the innate ridiculousness of human endeavour. Considering that this quality of humour is so present in Taoism more generally, it seems strange to me that all the versions of the Tao Te Ching (which is the oldest and most central text of classical Taoism, thought to be well over 2500 years old) are so poe-faced.

So... I decided to write a version in modern language, and with that sense of humour which is so important to my experience of Taoism. To come back to my original point, I wanted to give this version of the Tao Te Ching the flavour of Taoism as I experience it, because it has felt for a long time like something was missing from the versions I have read over the years. My hope in doing so is to keep a sense of the poetry and mystery which make the original so rich, while making it more accessible and fun to read and ponder for the next generation of Western wayward Taoists like myself.

None of this is intended as a criticism of those other texts. I've loved many versions of the Tao Te Ching over the years and I'm sure they have faithfully translated a complex and beautiful piece of esoteric prose poetry. That's awesome! And... because I am working from those translations but allowing my own perspective to colour my writing complete with influences from other faiths and poetry (most notably Sufi poetry), I am free to bend and re-shape the thing in a way true translators aren't. I would add however, that my intention has not been to bend it out of shape but to do my best to seek the essence of each chapter and express it in an accessible, loving, and deeply human way, with a touch of that sense of humour I find and love in Taoist tales.

In case you don't know what Taoism is...

If you don't know what Taoism is, there are lots of different faces of it in the modern world. Its origins are as the indigenous spirituality of China (before Buddhism arrived). I suspect that its roots are in the shamanic (native, tribal spiritual) traditions of China which then started to get recorded and therefore organised and passed on by rote over the generations until it gained a structured religious foundation.

Today, there are 2 basic branches: Religious Taoism which has a priesthood and gods and texts (much like most organised religions); and Esoteric Taoism which is the spiritual path most commonly associated with practices like Tai Chi and Chi Gung.

Most people will have encountered one of the core concepts of Taoism in the form of the 'Yin/Yang' symbol:

This represents balance more than anything else which is very important in Taoism. However you interpret light/dark, hot/cold, high/low, positive/negative, active/receptive, masculine/feminine, yin/yang, yes/no, it is about the balance of the polarities and their intimate relationship with each other. It also symbolises the idea that the light contains a seed of the dark and the dark contains a seed of the light. In this way it goes a step beyond balance as I see it, this becomes a symbol of integration which hints at the idea that while polarities seem to be opposed to each other, they are also mutually nourishing and interdependent. This tells us a lot about the deep heart of Taoism which is so intimately connected to the concepts of mystery and paradox. The world is essentially mysterious and behind every corner lays a paradox: an apparent contradiction which is true nonetheless, regardless of what linear logic says. You will see many such moments in the text to come – statements inviting us to embrace the mystery of life and contemplate paradox. In a way I think that lies at the heart of what the Tao Te Ching is: an invitation to let go of certainty, and by doing so, discover a more solid foundation than anything else can offer us: one thing never changes – the fact that everything changes.

A Fool's Guide to Effing the Ineffable

My

Tao

Te

Ching

A note on language: *I have used British English spelling because I'm British, I hope this isn't too distracting if you are American. I have roughly alternated gender when speaking about the 'Wise Fool' as I believe men and women are equally likely to exhibit mastery, wisdom, and foolishness.*

Chapter 1

I'm going to talk about something

I'll call it Tao (which means 'Way').

By Talking about it I'm only going to confuse matters,

But if I don't...

This will be a very short book.

Even by calling it "Tao" I've taken something

Amazing,

Limitless,

And wonderfully mysterious,

And reduced it to a 3 letter word.

Direct experience, no matter how confusing, is the real deal.

As soon as I give it a name it's just another thing.

Like...

The toaster,

Or the train,

Or Auntie Maureen,

Or the jelly mould.

Sometimes,

When we let go of our need to pin things down,

Our confusion can be very beautiful.

When we get obsessed with having all the answers

All we can see is the toaster.

Strangely: Beautiful confusion and the toaster come from the same place.

This place is called "The Dark."

It's so dark you can't see anything,

But if you want to understand

Then "The Dark"

Is the only place worth looking.

Chapter 2

When I say "I like **that** one,"

I'm also saying

I **don't** like the other one."

If I write a story with a good guy,

There's also got to be a villain.

Opposites create each other,

"Yes" to one means "no" to another.

In order to recognise light,

I have to see darkness.

For me to feel short,

Someone else must be tall.

'Later' only exists when we've had 'earlier'.

Knowing all this, the Wise Fool

Does stuff but is never do-ing,

Teaches people without anyone realising,

A "yes" is welcome,

A "no" is welcome.

She holds but never grasps,

She does what needs doing with no expectation of return[1].

Work is done for its own sake:

That's why it's so good.

---

[1] This line was inspired by a translation of a Hawaiian word which I discovered while studying Hawaiian Shamanism: Kahiau. It means 'To give generously from the heart with no expectation of return.' How awesome is it that they have a word for that?!

Chapter 3

If you put someone on a pedestal,

You make everyone else very small.

If you make "having stuff" the most
important thing

It's not surprising that people
will do anything to have the stuff.

The Wise Fool leads:

Not by telling people what to
think,

But by helping them to better
understand themselves.

Not by being the best,

But by getting the job done.

He helps people forget all about...

The toaster,

The train,

Auntie Maureen,

The jelly mould,

All the things that keep us tied to
one way of being.

He   ensures   that   everyone   gets
thoroughly confused!

When you stop trying to do the
doing,

The doing does itself.

Chapter 4

The Tao is like stone soup[2],

You start with nothing but everyone is fed.

It is like The Dark: Empty of visions but full of possibilities.

.

Soften your heart

And open your eyes:

Wonder-full and ordinary,

The Tao is The Source.

… How do you find the source of The Source?

---

2   There is an old story where a poor man sets up a cauldron in the town square with nothing but water and a stone in it. When asked what he's doing he says "Making stone soup."   Intrigued, everyone that comes by asks if they can offer anything for the pot in return for a taste once it's ready. With each person, the man says "I'm pretty much there but maybe a carrot would add something..." Or a potato, or a tomato, or a parsnip, or some herbs.... By the end of the day he has delicious soup enough to feed his family and everyone else too, when he started the day with only a pot full of water and a rock!

Chapter 5

The Tao is fiercely compassionate:

All things are equal.

The Wise Fool is fiercely compassionate:

He loves the good-guys, and the villains.

The Tao is like a drain-pipe,

Its emptiness is its value,

The more that flows the better.

Understanding, not over-talking.

Hold to the centre.

Chapter 6

Tao is the true Mother

Giving birth to all things...

The toaster,

The train,

Auntie Maureen,

The jelly mould,

All the wondrous multitudes.

Like a magic cupboard filled with endless treasures:

The key is always in your pocket.

Chapter 7

Tao goes on forever.

Why?

Because it was never born.

If you never start you don't have to finish.

The Wise Fool serves and therefore leads.

Unattached,

He is connected with all things.

He has emptied himself and so he is (ful)filled.

Chapter 8

The best things are like water:

Effortlessly nourishing all,

Flowing in the dark, forgotten places.

Just like the Tao.

In dwelling, connect with the land

In contemplation, soften and open

In relating, bring presence and compassion

In governing, offer freedom

In work, love what you do

In action, be just where you are

When you trust yourself, others can trust you too.

Chapter 9

Too much tea and not enough cup

Try too hard and sharp turns to blunt.

Chase after all the stuff, and true wealth runs through your fingers.

Chase approval,

And true love and happiness will be like the alarm clock on a winter morning:

Always just out of reach from the coziness of your duvet.

Commit to the work and walk away when it's done - you'll be happier that way.

Chapter 10

Can you collect yourself from the 1001 distractions and live completely from your heart?

Can you let yourself be soft, innocent, and open like a baby?

Can you get your glasses so clean you really see the world **as it is**?

With love and humility, can you lead people without telling them what to do?

Can you take responsibility without taking control?

Realising the nature of a thing, can you leave it alone (all-one)?

Creating and sustaining

Belonging without restriction

Meeting the world with "Thank you", not "Please"

Leading without commanding

These are the hearts' truths.

Chapter 11

A disk of wood can be fun,

But it's when we make a hole in the middle that we can use it as a wheel.

A ball of clay can be fun,

But it's when we scoop out the middle that we can use it as a bowl.

A giant box can be fun,

But it's when we cut a door that we can get inside.

The outer form – the thing – can be fun.

What's inside – the no-thing – is what gives it purpose.

Chapter 12

Looking blinds you,

Listening deafens you,

Tasting, tasting, tasting makes all things taste the same.

Seeking answers will tie your mind in knots.

Chasing all the shiny, sexy, yumminess will distract you from **The Way**.

So...

The Wise Fool enjoys the world through her senses,

But

Her actions are guided by the still, small voice at the centre of her being.

Don't be distracted by the jelly mould...

Chapter 13

You are going to lose and look a Fool time and time again – get used to it.

Life is painful and often hard work - deal with it.

It's the way of the world: as soon as you gain something you're at risk of losing it.

If you didn't have a body you couldn't feel pain or do work, but being human entails having a body.

Trying to deny these things is like trying to arm-wrestle the moon:

It's **way** bigger than you...and....

....It has no arms.

Accept the world on its terms and compassion will come naturally.

Love the world - and yourself as
part of it - just the way it is,
and you are truly ready to be
trusted.

Chapter 14

Look and you won't spot it,

Listen and you won't catch it,

Grab and you won't hold it.

Above there's no light,

Below there's no dark.

Indescribable, mysterious,

Path with no end.

Returning to the Dark no-thing,

Formless form,

Unimaginable image.

You can't pin it down and you can't
tell its story.

Follow the thread of it, there's no
beginning,

Turn around, there's no end.

Hold it in your heart,

It won't fit in your head.

It is the ancient myth of an ancient myth.

The Tao is the original original: Accept no substitutes.

Chapter 15

The oldest and wisest of Fools were mysterious, perceptive, poised, and totally present.

The depth of their wisdom plumbed the Dark-ness.

I can't tell you what they knew, but I can tell you how they acted:

Careful - like a man on thin ice!

Alert - like a child stealing cookies.

Courteous - like a fiancée meeting the in-laws.

Yielding - like chocolate on your tongue.

Simple - like a lump of wood.

Open - like a flower for a bee.

Unknown - like a box of cereal that **might** have a toy in it.

Can you wait and finish the cereal
to discover the toy?

Can you sit still until the moment
is ripe?

The   Wise   Fool   doesn't   chase
satisfaction.

Not chasing or seeking, he can sit
still and love what is.

Chapter 16

Let emptiness spread through your being,

Let peace be with you.

The toaster is bought, breaks and is discarded.

The train is popular, then becomes defunct.

Auntie Maureen is born, lives, gives inappropriate gifts to her nephews, and then dies.

The jelly mould is invented, finds greatest popularity as a car shape in orange plastic in the 1970's, then fades into cultural memory...

This is the natural way of things:

To come from darkness, spend time in the world, and return to darkness.

That's the Way of the world.

Knowing the Way of the world is wisdom.

Not knowing the Way of the world will lead to disappointment and pain.

Knowing the Way of the world you will meet it with an open heart,

With an open heart you will love and be loved,

Loving and being loved you will directly experience the mysterious wonder the world has to offer,

This mysterious wonder connects you with The Tao,

The Tao goes on forever.

Connected with The Tao, whether you live or die, you go on forever.

Chapter 17

The best acts are almost invisible,

The next best are known and loved,

The next: feared,

And finally, those that are despised.

As you trust, so shall you be trusted.

The Wise Fool leads by example

And when the job is done

Everyone celebrates

Their own success.

Chapter 18

When people lose their Way

Rules about morality and correct action are made.

When people stop trusting themselves,

They demand evidence before they will trust anyone.

When a group is divided

Loyalty and commitment need proving.

When a nation has lost its Way

Patriotism becomes a virtue.

Chapter 19

Give up holiness and wisdom,

And the world will be a better place.

Give up morality and rules about correct action,

And people will love each other and do the right thing.

Give up cleverness and profit,

And trickery and thieving will die out.

These three things are the wrapping, not the present.

Come back to centre

And listen to the still, small voice in your heart.

Chapter 20

Yes or No,

Good or Bad,

What's the difference?

Someone shouts "Terror!"

Should we all be terrified?

Everyone's excited!

Like toddlers at a party...

I am unmoved

Like a newborn before it learns to smile:

Open, undefined.

Everyone's rich and cosy,

I sit empty-handed

A ragged fool,

Nowhere is my home.

A fool to the core:

Everyone is bright,

I sit alone in Darkness.

Everyone has answers,

I only have questions.

I am adrift and rudderless on a
stormy sea.

I am the odd one out,

The stranger in the corner,

I am nourished

By the mystery.

Chapter 21

The Wise Fool is at one with The Tao. That's all.

The Tao is everywhere and no-where.

Not one but many, and none at the same time.

How can the Wise Fool be one with such mystery?

He just is.

The Tao is Dark, un-graspable, bright and clear.

How is the Wise Fool not confused?

He just is.

No more questions, this is how it has been since the beginning of time: It .....just is.

Chapter 22

Heart broken... open

Confusion and mystery lead to clarity.

To fill up, empty out.

Embrace dying to foster living.

Give to receive.

The Wise Fool lives from the Tao, listening to the still, small voice in her heart.

Quietly blossoming, people see her beauty.

Like the sun behind a cloud: Her brilliance is hidden but people feel her warmth.

When she makes a point, there's no arguing: she's got nothing to prove.

She offers an open heart and people
see themselves in her eyes.

With no ideas of good or bad she's
wonderful at everything!

When the ancients said "Embrace
dying to foster living," was that
crazy?

Surrender to the Way and find
yourself where you are:

Here and now

Here and now

Here and now

Stop trying to be something and be
something.

Chapter 23

Speak from the heart and then keep quiet.

Wind blows and then is gone,

Rain falls and then is gone,

It is natural for things to come and go,

Don't try and stretch things past their moment.

Surrender yourself to the Tao and the Tao will guide you.

Humble yourself before wisdom and you will be wise.

Embrace the pain of loss and even loss will be a source of life and beauty.

Trust like it's a wonderful game and others will join in the fun.

Chapter 24

Stretch up straight and stiff
trying to look powerful and you'll
lose contact with the ground that
gives you power.

Stretch and reach to get ahead and
you'll fall over your own feet.

Stretch your smile to show how
happy and radiant you are and
you'll look fixed and false.

Stretch and grasp and try to prove
yourself and all you'll prove is
your insecurity.

The Tao is not interested in your
efforts.

Just relax and be yourself.

Chapter 25

There was something that existed before everything...

It's still there:

Ever constant, never-ending, Dark within darkness, the still-point, and the chaos.

It is the mother of the 1001 things,

The source of the source.

For ease of reference I'll call it the Tao (which means The Way).

The Tao is awesome,

The Universe is awesome,

The Earth is awesome,

People are pretty awesome too!

People live within the Earth,

The Earth lives within the Universe,

The Universe lives within the Tao.

The Tao lives within the Tao:

It's the beginning of the beginning

And the end of the end.

Chapter 26

Loving the heavy

Will make your burdens light.

Stillness begets movement,

An immoveable spirit is the source
of a flexible mind,

So the Wise Fool is busy going
nowhere, constantly returning to
centre.

If a great leader only chases his
vision, he will be ungrounded.

No matter how delicious a dream is,
it won't fill your belly.

Embrace practicalities and every
day can be a dream come true.

Chapter 27

Skilful walkers tread lightly in the world,

Those who create great works know listening and stillness as well as action,

People who seek knowledge must keep asking questions – theories are there to be discovered, not invented.

So, the Wise Fool cultivates love for all people and all things.

There is light even in darkness… It may need encouraging.

How can we claim balance for ourselves if we do not help those who are wobbling?

What is that wobbling if it is not a striving for balance?

If you haven't realised the true value of both teacher and student, carers and those in need, the lover and the beloved...

Then...

You can be as clever as you like but you have lost your Way.

Darkness, Mystery: A Fool's Wisdom.

Chapter 28

Embodying male and female, the Tao will flow through you.

Residing in the darkness and the light, you are an example to the world.

With the capacity to stand

One foot in either pole,

Embodying the opposites and loving the beautiful confusion

You are a perfect vessel for the Tao.

The 1001 things that make up the world as we know it come from the Tao.

You can slice a block of wood to make shelves.

In pursuing my heart's work in the world I do different tasks.

The real magic lies in leaving the block uncut and the self undivided - while still getting the job done!

Chapter 29

If you have ideas about changing the world

Or think you can 'fix' it,

Think again.

The World is Sacred.

The World

Is Sacred.

It wasn't put here for you to meddle, and fiddle, and futz with it.

It's perfect just the way it is.

Be with it

Don't do to it,

Tinkering with it only disturbs the balance.

Within this great Mystery, there are:

Leaders and followers,

That which dances and that which sits,

The fire and the frost,

The strong and the weak,

Those who seek light and those who stand in shadow.

The Wise Fool walks the line.

She knows the extremes but doesn't stray towards them.

Water's wet, the sky is blue, **change happens**.

We don't need to manage it or make it.

Chapter 30

A true leader doesn't use force.

Violence begets violence.

The Wise Fool doesn't force matters;

Loving what is,

What is

Loves him.

The 1001 things will all come and go,

Live and then die.

The Tao is the only constant.

Chapter 31

All tools have a purpose

And weapons are made to harm.

To wield them against an-other

Should only be done as a last resort

When skill, luck, and ingenuity have been exhausted.

When weapons are drawn it should be with a calm, clear mind

But a heavy heart.

To enjoy harming others is to lose touch with your humanity.

If the Wise Fool must draw her sword

She does so filled with grief and compassion,

Attending to battle as she would attend a funeral.

Chapter 32

The Tao is unimportant,

Nothing special,

Easily ignored...

And...

It is a source of limitless power that could turn you into a super-hero!

Divine Paradox.

If great leaders could harness it

Everyone

Even your Auntie Maureen

Would do as they say.

It would rain jelly and ice-cream

And every day would be a party,

Like Heaven on Earth!

People would always listen to the still, small voices in their hearts and would just...

Do the right thing.

No laws necessary.

Until we reach such perfection

Having some rules helps.

But...

Even when saying "Stop!" you have to know when to stop.

Rules must serve life,

Life does not serve your rules.

All our lives are like little rivers

Flowing to the sea.

Chapter 33

To understand others takes a keen eye,

To understand yourself takes a wise heart.

To control others can be achieved with brute force.

To control yourself requires true strength of character.

Let go of desiring and wanting and chasing things...

And abundance might find you.

If you can stand at the gateway of the opposites,

Advancing on the path while standing your ground,

Then death will just be another
thing that happens

While you're busy living your life.

Chapter 34

The Tao flows through the world

Birthing

Nourishing

Loving.

It gives but asks nothing,

Creates but claims no credit,

Contains but never traps.

It's just there in the background.

Nothing special.

It is the ground of all being,

The great darkness we all return to.

Kind of a big deal.

The Wise Fool echoes the Tao:

He plods away in the background...

Accidentally   achieving   great
things.

Chapter 35

The Wise Fool, immersed in the Tao,

Has clear sight, a peaceful heart,
and beautifully simple actions.

Funky music or sweet-smelling food
will grab your attention.

The Tao is dull.

No melody,

No aroma.

But once you dip into it,

It's the juiciest game in town!

Chapter 36

To make something shrink,

First let it grow.

To make something weak,

First let it be strong.

If you wish something to leave,

Draw it into full presence.

This is called 'The Seed in the Darkness.'

The small will prevail against the great,

The humble will conquer the mighty.

You have nothing to prove with this:

Allow the mystery to unfold.

Chapter 37

The Tao never does anything

Yet through it the doings get done.

If leaders could learn this,

All things would go about their doings

And fall into their natural rhythms.

Out of these rhythms

The voice of the heart would emerge

And doings would become beings:

Simple, natural beings

Contented and at peace.

Imagine that!

The whole world contented and at peace.

Chapter 38

The Wise Fool is power-full,

Not power hungry.

The foolish man, power hungry,

Will never satisfy his appetite.

The Wise Fool does no doings

Yet from his being,

What's needed gets done.

The foolish man is full of doings,

So full the doings can never be done.

He who seeks to do good will always have one more thing to do.

He who seeks to do right has a never-ending task.

He who seeks justice will dive-in and get his hands dirty:

"You _will_ change and you'll like it!"

If we lose our Way (Tao) we'll try and be powerful,

If we don't feel powerful, we'll try and do good,

If we lose touch with what's good we'll try and do what's right,

If we lose touch with what's right we'll try and enforce justice.

Justice: the empty ritual that's left when we no-longer recognise rightness, goodness, power, and flow.

So.

The Wise Fool plumbs the depths;

He eats the nut and leaves the shell.

He doesn't try to <u>do</u> anything,

He is.

Chapter 39

Embodying your Way, your Tao,
brings a matchless integrity.

With integrity:

Magic Sparkles,

Earth supports,

The river runs,

Fire gives warmth,

Air breathes life,

Leaders lead the people.

Without integrity:

Magic is a trick,

Earth wobbles,

The river pools and stagnates,

Fire destroys,

The air is poisoned,

Leaders control the people.

The Wise Fool loves all things in their place:

The low for being foundations

And the high for reaching the heavens.

She stands in the mud with her head in the clouds.

She is noticed for her beauty but valued for her presence.

Chapter 40

The nature of the Tao is a constant returning,

Returning,

Returning.

The Way of the Tao is a constant Yielding,

Yielding,

Yielding.

The toaster, the train, Auntie Maureen, the jelly mould – all the 1001 things of the world – they all come into Being.

Being doesn't have to come into anything: it never left.

Chapter 41

The Tao:

Wise folk embody it,

Average Joe swallows some whole and
leaves the rest,

Dumb folk laugh and dismiss it.

If there wasn't laughter and
dismissal then we'd know it wasn't
the real deal.

So it is said:

To find the light you have to enter
the Dark,

To get better, things must get
worse,

To have power, you must embrace
vulnerability.

The pure may not seem perfect,

Simple doesn't mean easy,

To find order you must embrace chaos.

Structure brings freedom.

The greatest beauty is unrefined,

The greatest love is not attached,

True wisdom seems foolish.

The Tao is nowhere to be found,

But it's right before your eyes.

Chapter 42

Tao births one – the source.

One births two – light and dark.

Two births three – "not this, not that, but the other."

Three births four – Earth, the rivers, fire, the air.

Four births everything else – the 1001 things that make up the universe.

Every-thing has light and dark, yes and no, yin and yang.

Combine these opposites and you have a dynamic balance,

Each challenging and supporting the other.

When they are integrated, Yin and Yang nourish each other.

Most people fear loss,

The Wise Fool loses fear.

Chapter 43

The softest things

Flow around

The hardest things.

The insubstantial

Can penetrate the heart

Of the impenetrable.

No need to try so hard.

Just being with him people learn
without being taught:

That's how the Wise Fool does it.

Chapter 44

Would you rather people know who you are, or that you know who you are?

Would you rather be wealthy or abundant?

Would you rather win or lose?

If you embrace loss then the promise of gain will not tempt you from your Way.

Make contentment your habit.

Love the world just the way it is,

And the world will love you back.

Chapter 45

Perfectly imperfect.

So full, the space is endless.

Walking straight ahead

Down a crooked path.

The Wise Fool's precise footsteps seem casual, even clumsy to the untrained eye.

With nothing to prove

Move when you need to move,

Be still when you need stillness,

And face the world with a quiet mind and an open heart.[3]

---

3 Thanks to my friend Andy Bradley of Frameworks4Change for the phrase 'Quiet mind, Open Heart.' Check out his TEDx talk on 'The Compassion Gap' - it's awesome!

Chapter 46

When people are walking their Way,
living in the Tao

They prepare for work.

When people stray from their Path

They prepare for war.

There's nothing worse than living
in fear,

Facing all of life as a battle

In a dog-eat-dog world.

When you can embrace the work and
let go of the struggle

The world is a friendly place

And contentment will blossom in
your heart.

Chapter 47

You don't have to travel the world to love it.

You don't have to go searching to find yourself.

The more intellectual baggage you gather,

The heavier your load on the path to wisdom.

The Wise Fool:

Rests his legs but stretches his heart,

Closes his eyes but opens his mind,

Is always the same but changes the world.

Chapter 48

Being 'Learned' means gathering knowledge.

Being Wise means letting it all go,

Emptying out,

Becoming like a hollow pipe:

What is needed flows through you,

You don't do the doings but the doings get done.

If you want to be powerful,

Get out of the way.

Anyone who's too full of themselves has no space for power.

Chapter 49

The Wise Fool has a mind like the
town square:

Everyone wanders through it.

She welcomes good people and bad
people,

She welcomes the trustworthy and
the faithless,

Her goodness and trust are governed
by her choices, not yours.

The Wise Fool melts into the world.

Open like a child,

Loving like a parent.

Chapter 50

The Wise Fool has only one true teacher.

He teaches how to live

Fully

Awesomely

Heart open,

And soul laid bare.

He teaches how to live

With no illusions,

No resistance,

And no fear.

He teaches how to live

Vulnerably invulnerable,

So courageously loving

That no disaster can shake you

And no enemy harm you.

What teacher could teach even the
Wise so much about living?

Only Death my friend

Only Death.

Chapter 51

Everything

Every...

Thing

Is born from the Tao.

Like flowers on a tree

They bud

Blossom

Fruit

And fall

To nourish the roots, returning to the source.

That's why all things love and honour the Tao:

It's natural, why wouldn't they?!

To have but not to own,

To hold but not to grasp,

To lead but not command

    — This is real power.

That's why the Tao is sometimes
called 'Great Mystery':

Coz it's mysterious

And it's great.

Chapter 52

The Tao is the original original,

The source of the source.

All things flow out of it.

Every thing is born from it,

You've met the 1001 children,

Now meet the Mother.

When you've really understood the children, you'll know the Mother too.

Knowing the Great Mother,

When your time comes

To return to her embrace

Your heart will be at peace.

If you can close the door to the world for the sake of quietude,

But open the door to the world for the sake of love

Then life will nourish you.

If you open the door to the world for the sake of busyness,

But close the door to the world for the sake of protection

Then life will trouble you, and you will become deadened, a stranger eve to yourself.

Gazing into the Dark births vision.

Opening yourself to the world births strength.

Trust your own light to show you The Way.

These are the practices for always (all-ways) living

Chapter 53

The Way

Is humble,

Arrogance will lead you astray.

The Way

Is the path of your life,

Why does everyone want short-cuts?

They only speed your journey to the
end!

When all we see is the rich getting
richer,

The poor getting poorer,

Wealth being flaunted, stolen, and
protected,

Something...

Has gone wrong.

Surely

<u>That</u> way

Is not

The Way.

Chapter 54

With the Tao as your ground you'll be unshakeable,

With the Tao as your home you'll be safe.

Your ancestors will always be with you, you are never alone.

When you follow your Way, you have authenticity.

When your family follows their Way, you have true belonging.

When your community follows its Way, you have a sense of purpose.

When your country follows its Way, you have a sense of identity.

When the whole world follows its Way, then magic can happen!

How do I know?

Because...

That's The Way! (...things work)

Chapter 55

Embodying The Way

Power flowing

Is like being a new-born baby.

The baby is small, vulnerable, soft
and open,

Yet it is fearless, instinctive,
and its grip is naturally strong.

The baby doesn't know why it
becomes excited — it just does.

Now that's true vitality!

The baby can shout and cry all day
without ever tiring.

Now that's real stamina!

The Wise Fool lets power flow
through her.

The Wise Fool 'does' nothing.

She gets out of the way and into
The Way.

Things happen.

Flowing

Keeps going.

Death is a full stop.

When you allow your heart to flow,
your spirit becomes eternally
young.

Chapter 56

Anyone who says they can tell you
The Way doesn't know it.

Anyone who knows The Way doesn't
tell it.

Be silent,

Be dull,

Be simple,

Be soft,

Be extra ordinary,

Then you will be extraordinary.

No-one will be able to tell you
what to do,

Or manipulate you,

Or mess with you,

Or push you.

Yes or No,

Love or Hate,

Pull or Push:

You'll be unshakeable.

Extra-ordinary but wonder-full.

Chapter 57

In peacetime embrace harmony,

In conflict embrace discord.

Let go of what you <u>think</u> you <u>should</u>
be doing,

And what's needed will get done.

The more you tell people what to
do, the less they know for
themselves.

The more you try and fix things,
the more there is to fix.

If you try and impose <u>anything</u>,
people will struggle against it.

The Wise Fool says:

"I stop telling what to do and ask
what needs doing.

I stop fixing things and ask how I can help.

I stop planning and just keep asking.

I stop becoming and practice being:

Nowhere to go

Nothing to 'do'

Simple pleasure!"

Chapter 58

When leaders embrace mystery and ask questions

The followers are happy, engaged.

When leaders come up with bright ideas,

The followers will pick holes in them.

Good intentions become bad results.

A desire to help becomes unwanted interference.

Teaching values becomes enforcing dogma.

It's a crazy world!

So the Wise Fool

Guides without telling,

Offers without imposing.

He brings the Darkness so other
people can shine.

Chapter 59

When you want to be of service

There is nothing like meekness.[4]

Shut your mouth

And open your mind.

Throw away all your clever solutions.

You can only do this when you trust yourself.

When you trust yourself you can accomplish anything,

You become limitless and masterful,

A natural Leader.

---

4 We tend to think of 'meek' as meaning small and weak but the original meaning of 'meek' has been described as like a powerful horse, well trained. Now I get why the meek shall inherit the earth!

To govern, embrace The Mother:
nurturing and unconditional.

Your love must have deep roots

If you want your compassion to
last.

Chapter 60

If you want to learn to lead big groups of people

Practice by cooking a small fish.

Both tasks require constant and fierce attention, but minimal and gentle intervention.

Embrace your Way

Here and Now

And the ghosts of your past need not bother you.

You'll still have your demons in the cupboard,

Just like everyone else

But they won't rule your thoughts and dictate your actions.

Your wisdom will flow and call forth the wisdom in others.

The Dark corners of your soul are
like animals:

Cage them and beat them and they'll
bite you at every opportunity.

Free them and love them and they'll
be your best companions in life's
wild places.

Chapter 61

Greatness is like the sea:

Everything flows towards it.

Sustaining greatness is not about rising high,

It is about sinking down -

Rivers don't flow uphill!

True greatness embraces the Tao

And kisses the ego goodbye.

Mistakes become opportunities to learn,

Failure becomes a gateway to success,

Enemies become allies.

When you're willing to be low, base, simple and foolish,

Greatness will seek you out all by
itself.

Chapter 62

The Tao is the heart of all things.

Wise Fools live there,

And anyone is welcome to visit.

You can pay people to do things for you

With trade or money or praise,

But the best things are offered out of love.

So when a leader steps out to lead,

Don't offer glory, or money, or even praise to their cause.

Just turn up with an open heart: the gateway to the Tao.

Why do Wise Fools live in the Tao?

Whatever you need can be found there,

Whatever burdens you carry can be laid to rest.

Where else could you go but Here?

Chapter 63

Achieve but don't try

Consider but don't think

Approach the large and complex like it is small and simple.

When faced with curses, offer blessings.

Heroic deeds begin with small, simple acts.

Overnight success blossoms out of many years of practice.

The Wise Fool never tries to be great, she just is.

She plods her Way towards enlightenment,

And creates magic one dull task at a time.

Embracing the difficult and boring,
the Wise Fool never tires

Because everything brings her joy.

Chapter 64

Things that never move are easy to find.

Things that often move are easy to change.

Things that cannot flex are easy to break.

Things that constantly flex are easy to disrupt.

Be the cause, not the effect.

Get clear before you get in a mess.

The great oak tree grew from a tiny acorn,

And the journey of your dreams begins right where you are.

Here and Now

Here and Now

Here and Now

Wading in the river

If you try and push it, you'll
create turbulence but it will flow
no faster.

Try and grasp it and it'll trickle
through your fingers.

Knowing this, the Wise Fool

Flows with the river,

Tries not to try,

Works not to work,

Remembers to forget,

Takes pleasure in the finishing
touches as well as the opening
flourish.

He loves enough not to interfere.

He embraces what is.

Chapter 65

It is said

That in a time outside time,

And a place beyond place,

Wise Fools

Were the leaders and the teachers.

They didn't teach people to know things,

They taught people no-things.

People who think they know are difficult to guide.

People who know they don't know ask all the right questions.

If you want to learn, teach, or lead,

Don't be clever or showy.

Intellect blinds,

Enquiry illuminates.

If you're willing to be simple,
foolish, unknowing,

Then you can teach, guide, or lead

Anyone

Until...

They know The Way for themselves.

Chapter 66

The seas and lakes are low,

Yet all the streams and rivers pay them tribute.

Understanding this, the Wise Fool knows:

To rise, sink

To be admired, be humble

To lead, serve.

The Wise Fool is powerful

But no-one feels overpowered.

She's in the lead but no-one feels lead-on.

Everyone loves her.

Even when she wins, no-one feels beaten.

Chapter 67

Many people call me a dreamer and an idealist.

They say 'Real Life' is hard.

I'd say that if you remember your dreams and re-connect with your ideals, life may get a little easier.

Three things are precious to me:

Foolishness, Darkness, and Love.

The Wise Fool has nothing to prove and so he is at peace.

The Dark is limitless and un-knowable so true knowing may be found there.

Love connects all things.

Tune out Love and you are lost.

Tune into Love and while you may still be lost, you will have companions on the path:

The lovers, the dreamers and me[5].

---

[5] This line is a quote from a Kermit the Frog Song in the original Muppet Movie. Really! You should check it out. It is profound and beautiful ☺

Chapter 68

The best aren't trying to win:

True sportsmen seek to play,

True warriors seek peace,

True leaders seek to be of service.

This is non-competition.

Only the terminally insecure need to 'beat' their opponents or 'destroy enemies.'

Bring your best game and honour your opponent as a collaborator in inspiring excellence:

Stand for, not against.

The spirit of play is essential in living your Way.

Chapter 69

The Warrior says:

"Rather than charging, receive your
opponent and invite them in.

Don't struggle for an inch when you
can yield a foot."

This is called

'Getting somewhere by going nowhere'

Asserting without aggressing,

Loving them to death!

There is nothing worse than
fighting someone you can't get hold
of,

And there is no greater loss than
the loss of your humanity.

Judging the outcome of battles is complex and the victor may be the person who gave most away.

When 2 great forces meet it is not a battle of strength,

It is a battle of surrender.

By releasing the outcome you embrace possibility.

Chapter 70

Everything the Wise Fool says is straight-forward,

Her actions are simple.

And yet....

People find her confusing

Her actions obscure and complex.

Ancient wisdom can be hard to digest with a modern mind.

The finest jewels are sometimes hidden in Dark places.

Chapter 71

Any knowledge can be poisoned by
your arrogance.

It is said that with great power
comes great responsibility.

So too, with great knowledge should
come great humility.

If you are not humbled by all that
you have learned

Then you may have learned much

But you have understood little.

You have come down with a bad case
of believing your own hype!

The Wise Fool is his own doctor:

By knowing his own foolishness he
is inoculated against the idiocy of
the "Expert."

Chapter 72

Everything serves a purpose.

The Ego helps us meet the world safely,

Fear helps us to know when there's danger,

Knowledge helps us live and work intelligently.

Therefore the Wise Fool:

Embraces the ego but doesn't let it run the show,

Listens to her fear without letting it squash her passion,

And teaches by helping people uncover their own deep knowing.

Chapter 73

Courage can save your life,

Foolhardiness can end it.

Who knows which is which in the mess and muddle of life?

The Tao flourishes without competing,

Answers without speaking,

Gathers without calling.

It acts simply, and simply acts.

Its nature is generous and spacious

But nothing escapes its notice.

Chapter 74

Death is coming

For you

And everyone and everything you have ever known.

It's normal to have feelings about that:

Fear and grief and sadness.

But if you let those feelings rule you,

You're as good as dead already.

To try and do-away with death,

Or change change

Is like picking up the Great Mother's knife:

You're bound to cut yourself

And that is gonna hurt real bad...

Chapter 75

Greed gives birth to poverty,

Manipulation gives birth to resentment,

Abuse of power gives birth to rebellion.

This is true in nations and it's also true in you.

If you allow your intellect to become a petty tyrant

Inventing reasonable reasons to relinquish your deepest dreams,

Then don't be surprised if:

Your soul is impoverished,

Your heart filled with resentment,

And your body in rebellion.

Chapter 76

The living are warm, soft, flowing;

Corpses are cold, hard, and rigid.

In nature, juicy vibrancy is a sign of life,

Brittle dullness a sign of death.

So if you practice being warm, soft, and flowing you will master the kung-fu of life.

If you practice being cold, hard and rigid you will master the kung-fu of death.[6]

---

6 'Kung-fu' is used to refer to martial arts but the 3 most common translations I have come across are: Skill, skilful movement, and 'time and hard work.' So really it is just one aspect of the martial arts. The kung-fu of death might sound cool to any hard-core-ninja-army-fighter types out there but the implication in 'kung-fu' is that what you practice, you become. I'm fine with dying when it's my time but I'm not keen on quickening the process through practice!

The brittle and dull will be broken
and cast aside,

The juicy and vibrant will thrive.

Chapter 77

The Way of the Tao

Is like bending a bow to shoot an arrow:

To get the job down you have to bend the top down and the bottom up.

There's balance.

What is high sinks,

What is low rises,

And everyone feels their value as they move closer together for a common purpose.

All too often our human world is like the opposite of Robin Hood:

Robbing from the poor

To give to the rich,

And crap with a bow and arrow!

Aligned with the Tao, the Wise Fool
is endlessly abundant:

She gives generously from the heart
with no expectation of return

And achieves without arrogance.

She is in the middle of the bow -

Seeing everyone as equal

And riding the arrow to her target.

Chapter 78

Nothing is as soft and flowing as water.

And yet...

There's nothing like it for wearing away the hard, the rigid.

Soft overcomes hard,

The flowing will defeat the rigid.

The evidence of this is all around us

But no-one seems to take any notice.

The Wise Fool

Keeps his centre

In the midst of the storm.

His vulnerability is the guardian

of his open heart.

.　.　.　.

That last bit sound strange?

Paradox is the way of things

So if a truth doesn't confuse you
at least a little bit....

It's probably not the truth!

(Or you haven't understood it yet)

Chapter 79

Blame is highly contagious.

If you pick it up

You'll pass it on,

And on,

And on.

The   Wise   Fool   knows   that
accountability can only be taken,

You can't force it on anyone.

People of true power do what they
say they will and honour their
word.

People of false power say what
should be done and require a
multitude of promises.

The Tao, like all of nature, is morally neutral,

It always supports the good guys.[7]

---

7   If you're struggling with these last few lines, see the previous chapter... I'm not saying it'll make sense but it might at least give context!

Chapter 80

The Wise Fool dreams of a place

Where

People love their work

So much

They won't let you make it easier.

Where

People love their homes

So much

They won't accept a holiday.

Where

There is a toaster but no-one uses it

A train but no-one goes on it

An Auntie Maureen but no-one listens to her gossiping

A jelly mould but people carve the

jelly by hand just for the hell of it!

The Wise Fool dreams

Of simple pleasures

And loving relationships.

The Jones's can flaunt their wealth

And angels can whisper divine secrets just over the border with Heaven.

No-one's keeping up, and no-one's listening.

When you have found your Way, your Home

You don't need anything else.

Chapter 81

The truth is rarely glamorous

And the glamorous is rarely true.

The Wise question

But never doubt.

The learned doubt

But never question.

The Wise Fool gives it all away:

She rejoices in other people's pleasure

And giving is how she receives.

The Tao creates wealth without making poverty.

The Wise Fool is masterful without being superior.

My Tao Te Ching

Enjoyed this book?

Check out my website and sign up for my newsletter to get access to members' resources and hear about future books and online courses before anyone else:

www.fudoshin.org.uk/newsletter

My Tao Te Ching online course coming soon...

AKNOWLEDGEMENTS

Without being too grand I do feel that I have some people to thank in this book. First of all is always my wife and son for being with me through the eccentric life I have chosen for myself and inflict on them - thank you for your patience and faith, I love you.

Many teachers have influenced me deeply over the years but for the work of this book Sensei Steve Rowe has to be top of the list for being my first serious martial arts teacher and for introducing me to the inimitable Tao Te Ching in the first place! Sensei Tom Maxwell also played a big part in my martial education so thanks must go to him as well. I continue in my Taoist adventure now with Dylan Newcomb whose work is a new inspiration. Thank you all.

There are many other teachers and many companions on the path but in order not to bore you all to tears here are some thanks in no particular order: Syd, Alan, Robbie, Niamh, Alex, Trish, Simon, Kate, Kate, Jamie, Claire, Clare, Mark, Tess, Leanne, and many others! Thanks ☺ With Love.

ABOUT THE AUTHOR

Francis Briers has been exploring the mind-body connection for 20 years and facilitating learning for groups and individuals for 15. He trained originally as an actor but then ran away from the circus to find his home. Along the way he studied martial arts (to black belt and instructor standard), Taoism, shamanism, bodywork, various spiritual and wisdom traditions from around the world, and was ordained as an Interfaith Minister and spiritual counsellor. He is a writer and facilitator working with Embodiment, Conscious Leadership, Compassion, and Sustainability with organisations. He runs public workshops and online trainings on personal and spiritual development.

He lives in East Grinstead, UK, with his beloved and beautiful wife and son. He likes chocolate, the view of trees out his shed window, and being by the sea when it's stormy.

www.francisbriers.com

34341764R00093

Made in the USA
Charleston, SC
07 October 2014